NINTENDO ®
ACTION GAMES

NIN TEN DO

ACTION GAMES

BY CHRISTOPER LAMPTON

THE MILLBROOK
PRESS
BROOKFIELD, CT.

Cataloging-in-Publication Data

Lampton, Christopher

Nintendo action games. Brookfield, CT,
Millbrook Press, 1991.
72 p.; ill.:
Includes index.
1. Video games. 2. Electronic toys.
I. Title. 794.8 LAM
ISBN: 1-878841-26-2

NINTENDO® ACTION GAMES is not licensed by
or in any way affiliated with Nintendo of America, Inc.

Nintendo® is a registered trademark of
Nintendo of America, Inc.

TRADEMARKS AND COPYRIGHTS

CONTENTS

NINTENDO® ACTION GAMES

INTRODUCTION

Zap! Pow! Zowee!

Grab your game controller and get ready to have the most fun that you can have sitting down. It's time to play Nintendo!

The Nintendo Entertainment System—NES, for short—is a home video game machine that plays cartridge games of near arcade quality. Ever since it was imported from Japan in the mid-1980s, it has been one of the hottest selling entertainment systems both in the United States and around the world.

This book is intended for Nintendo players who want to improve their scores at the games they're already playing or who just want to decide what games they want to play. In the pages that follow, we'll review twelve different video games, some of them recent, some of them classics. We've tried to give you the information you need to decide which of these games you'd like and to help you play better and longer once you've started.

The games in this book are action games. A companion volume to this book features role-playing games. What's the difference?

A lot of Nintendo games combine elements of arcade action and role-playing in a single package, and it's difficult to put them in one category or the other. The author of this book has used his own judgment as to which games should be included, but you certainly have the right to disagree.

Basically, an action game is any video game that emphasizes fast action and quick thinking over puzzle-solving and complicated plot. Check out *Contra,* for example.

Role-playing games, on the other hand, are more like novels or movies in which the player gets to be the main character or characters. The characters actually develop and grow in the course of the game, becoming stronger and smarter and better at what they do. There are elements of role-playing in many of the games in this book, but the emphasis here is on fast action. The games in *Nintendo Role-Playing Games,* a companion to this book, have plenty of action, but there the emphasis is instead on puzzle-solving and plot.

Nintendo games are played with a device called a *game controller,* which you hold in your hands while you play. There are four buttons on the game controller, labeled SELECT, START, A, and B, plus a directional controller with arrows pointing up, down, left, and right. In different games these buttons can do different things, but in most games you'll find that they work like this: the left and right buttons cause a tiny character on the screen to move left and right; the A button makes the character jump; the B button enables

the character to use a weapon. The START key pauses the game, and the SELECT button activates a special menu. At the beginning of the game, the SELECT button is used for choosing items from menus on the screen and the START key is used to start the game.

Sometimes these buttons can be used in special combinations to make your character perform fancy tricks, such as jumping and fighting at the same time or even grabbing another character by the hair. These tricks are explained in the manual that comes with the game, though we'll give you a few of them here.

Most action games are divided up into a series of stages or levels, each of which has its own scenery and its own set of villains and monsters for your character to fight against. Sometimes these levels and stages are divided up into sublevels and substages. At the end of each level, and often at the end of a sublevel, you'll encounter a "boss"—commonly either a male character or a monster—whom you have to get past in order to complete the level. The boss is usually the toughest villain on the level, but there is sometimes a special trick you can use to get past him. We'll tell you a few of those tricks in this book.

The descriptions of the games in this book are divided into seven parts. Here are the names of the parts and an explanation of what you will find in each one:

AT A GLANCE

A quick description of what the game is about, so that you'll know whether you want to read more.

QUICK REVIEW

A brief assessment of the game so that you'll know what the author of this book thought of it. We can tell you in advance, though, that all of the games included in this book are considered by the author to be good.

HOW IT WORKS

A longer explanation of what the game is about and how to play it. Here you'll find a description of how to use the controller as well as a summary of the game and the various levels of play.

TIPS & TRICKS

This is the part for players who want to play better. We'll give you hints on how to improve your playing tech-nique, as well as specific clues on how to get past particularly thorny obstacles in the game.

BACKDOORS & PASSWORDS

Some games contain special "back doors." What's a back door (besides another way of getting out of a house)? It's a secret trick provided by the programmer who wrote the game, often used by the programmer or the game testers to check out the game before it is released. A typical back door requires that you press a sequence of buttons on the controller during the opening screens of the game. The effect of pressing these buttons is often to give your character extra lives or to allow you to enter special game screens that you can't see any other way.

A password, on the other hand, is a sequence of letters and numbers that some games will print on the screen when you quit playing, so that you can restart the game at the same high level without having to play through the lower levels again. We'll give you a few passwords that will let you sneak a peek at the higher levels of certain games, but not so many that they'll spoil your fun in discovering others for yourself.

FASCINATING FACTOIDS

If we know any interesting trivia about the game or the characters in the game or the programmer who wrote the game, or even the music in the game, we'll pass it on here.

Have we whetted your video game appetite yet?

If so, why are you still reading the introduction? Turn the page, and let the games begin!

THE ADVENTURES OF LOLO 2

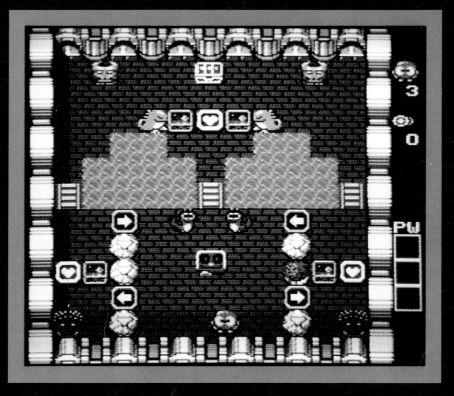

AT A GLANCE

Manufactured by HAL America. A cuddly creature has to find his way through a mazelike castle to rescue his kidnapped girlfriend. Lots of puzzles, strange creatures, and a dash of action.

QUICK REVIEW

The best strategy game around. For players who like to use their brains as well as their game controllers.

HOW IT WORKS

You are Lolo, a funny little blue furball with big eyes. You have to work your way through room after room and floor after floor of the king of Eggerland's castle to find your fellow furballs, who are prisoners, and set them free. One of those prisoners is your girlfriend, Lala.

Use the directional controller to move Lolo north, south, east, and west. To complete a room, you have to collect all of the square-shaped Heart Framers, then take a jewel from the Jewel Box. To make your job more difficult, each room is chockful of strange creatures who want to eat you, zap you, push you into corners you can't get out of, or just get in your way. There are also one-way passages and nearly impassable rivers standing between you and your goal.

The B button lets you start a room all over again if you find yourself in a hopeless situation, which you often will. But it will cost you a life. Fortunately, the game allows unlimited lives, called *continues*. You'll get a password when the game is over so that you can start at the same level the next time.

Every now and then you'll find a Heart Framer that will give you special powers. One of these powers is the ability to turn your enemies into eggs! A number appears on the right-hand side of the screen telling you that you have a special power. You can use that power by pressing the A button. Another special power allows you to reverse one-way passages.

When your opponents turn into eggs, you can push them around and even knock them off the screen with a second shot. But watch out! After a few seconds, the eggs will hatch and turn back into the same creature you thought you had gotten rid of—even if you shot them off the screen!

Some eggs will float when pushed into water. Lolo can climb on top of a floating egg and get a ride downstream. In fact, this is the only way to cross rivers and lakes. Alas, if the egg sinks before it reaches its destination, Lolo will go down with it!

Lolo can push the square-shaped Emerald Framers out of his way, a talent that proves useful for trapping his foes or blocking their attacks. Boulders and bushes, which Lolo can't push, are also good for blocking attacks. But beware. Some bad guys can zap Lolo right through the bushes!

TIPS & TRICKS

- The secret to solving many of the rooms in *Lolo* is to move things into the right places in the right order. Move Emerald Framers to block attacks, save your special powers for just the right moment, and be careful not to get zapped along the way!
- Never move an Emerald Framer farther than you have to. You might get it into a position where you can't move it again, even if you need to.
- Here's a set of hints for each of the first ten rooms in *Lolo 2*. If you're having trouble getting started, this should get you on your way:

Floor 1, Room 1: This is the easiest room of all. Just collect all the hearts but one, turn a lizard into an egg, and push him out of the way to reach the last Heart Framer. Then grab the jewel from the Jewel Box and head for the door.

Floor 1, Room 2: More practice at turning the enemy into eggs. Watch out for those Skulls, though. When you get the last heart, they'll come to life—and head straight for Lolo! See if you can get out of this room with at least one special power left.

Floor 1, Room 3: Now things get tough. This is probably the hardest room on the first floor, and you should give yourself a pat on the back when you figure it out. Trapping Alma is easy; in fact, she'll throw herself right into the trap! But getting the Heart Bracers is harder. You'll have to move the Emerald Framers into exactly the right positions before you can make your way past them. HINT: Push some of the Emerald Framers up and down and some of them sideways.

Floor 1, Room 4: Move fast! The little green Leepers like nothing better than to run up to you and fall fast asleep. Unfortunately, nothing can move a sleeping Leeper. And, if you let them get on all sides of you or trap you in a corner, there's no way out. You'll have to press the B button and start again. Fortunately, once a Leeper goes to sleep, he can't follow you. You'll finish this room in a few seconds if you finish it at all!

Floor 1, Room 5: Meet the Medusas! These snake-haired creatures will zap you if they can get a straight shot with

no obstacles in the way. Fortunately, they can't move, so push the Emerald Framers where they'll protect you from danger. And don't let those pesky Rockies shove you into a corner!

Floor 2, Room 1: Congratulations! You've made it to the second floor! As a reward, you get one of the easiest rooms in the game. There are two one-way passages that you don't even have to go down and one Rocky who will try to push you into a corner you can't get out of. Stay as far from Rocky as you can get and you'll be done in no time.

Floor 2, Room 2: This is one of those rooms where the exact order in which you do things is important. There are two Medusas and a lot of Emerald Framers. You'll need to move all the Emerald Framers into the right positions before you can safely gather all the hearts and get the jewel.

Floor 2, Room 3: The Skulls are your main problem here. You'll have two egg shots when you're finished gathering the hearts, and you'll need both of them. Move the framers so that only two of the Skulls can chase you after the last heart is taken. And be on your toes. When a Skull gets on your trail, it can move fast!

Floor 2, Room 4: There are three Rockies in this room, two moving up and down on the sides and one moving clockwise around the center. Don't let two Rockies gang up on you at once! Stay on the opposite side from the center Rocky so that he can't get your scent and keep darting in and out to grab the hearts protected by the other two Rockies. Again, don't get backed into a corner!

Floor 2, Room 5: This room takes patience. There's only one Medusa, but you'll have to move the Emerald Framers into exactly the right positions, in exactly the right order, before you can get that last Heart Framer away from her. The other Heart Framers are easy to get. Grab them up before you begin the tough part. There are two solutions to getting the last Heart Framer; one is a mirror image of the other.

BACKDOORS & PASSWORDS

If you're still having trouble getting through the first two floors, the password for the first room on the third floor is PYPL. Use it to look around. But if you can't solve the first floor, don't expect the third floor to be easier!

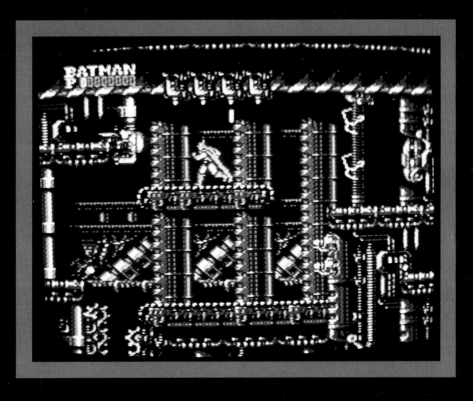

AT A GLANCE

Manufactured by Sunsoft. The Caped Crusader pursues his archenemy, the Joker, through the shadowy streets and towers of Gotham City.

QUICK REVIEW

The best graphics and music in any Nintendo program to date and some first-rate jumping and fighting action!

HOW IT WORKS

Use the directional controller to move Batman left and right. The A button makes him jump, the B button fires his current weapon. The default weapon is Batman's fists, but he'll pick up other weapons as he works his way through the hordes of attacking enemies. Push the SELECT button to toggle through all of the weapons that Batman is holding. They'll include a boomerang, a pistol, and the deadly dirk.

A special capability of the Nintendoized *Batman* is the Wall Jump. You'll need lots of practice to pull this one off. Press A for a normal jump. Then, when Batman hits a wall, hit the B button. He'll cling to the wall for a second, then kick off in the other direction. If there are two walls close enough together, Batman can climb up the shaft between them!

The game is divided into five stages, each of which is divided into smaller substages. In the first stage, Batman pursues the Joker's henchmen into a deserted construction site. Scaling girders and walls, Batman is attacked by robots and flying villains.

In the second stage, Batman searches for the Joker himself in the Axis Chemical factory. He must avoid electrocution from sparking power coils and must leap across deadly pools of acid.

The third stage takes the Caped Crusader through underground passageways, along pipes, and past dangerous machinery. In the fourth stage, Batman penetrates the Joker's hideout, a laboratory filled with sinister equipment. Finally, in the fifth stage, he confronts the Clown Prince of Crime himself at the top of the towering Gotham City Cathedral.

TIPS & TRICKS

- Learn to do the Wall Jump as soon as possible. In Stage 1, Part 2, you'll find a shaft heading straight up between two walls. There you can practice the jump with minimal interference from the Joker's minions.
- Study the differences between Batman's weapons. Special tokens that the Dark Knight Detective picks up while fighting villains give him energy for using weapons, but some weapons require more energy than others.
- For the easiest foes, use the boomerang. It works over a longer distance than Batman's fists and uses less energy than any of his other special weapons.
- The dirk shoots both higher and lower than other weapons. It's especially useful for fighting flying villains.
- The big boss at the end of Stage 1 is Killer Moth, who swoops down at you from the sky and pelts you with fireballs. It's not as tough as it looks. Move to one of the two sides of the screen; it won't be able to hit you there. Then, when it flies near the ground, zap it with the dirk!
- The Cybernoid boss at the end of Stage 3 has an electric arm that will fry Batman if he lets it touch him. Use the down arrow button to make Batman crouch under the Cybernoid's swing.

FASCINATING FACTOIDS

Batman, the creation of cartoonist Bob Kane, first appeared in the pages of Detective Comics in 1939. The *Batman* television series, which debuted on ABC in 1966, was one of the few prime time television shows ever to appear two nights each week. Usually, a story would begin on one night and be completed on the other night, leaving viewers in suspense for the two or three days in between!

The 1989 movie based on the adventures of the Caped Crusader had the largest opening weekend of any movie in history and was a very popular film. Surprisingly, it was released on videotape less than five months after it opened in the theaters.

BUBBLE
BOBBLE

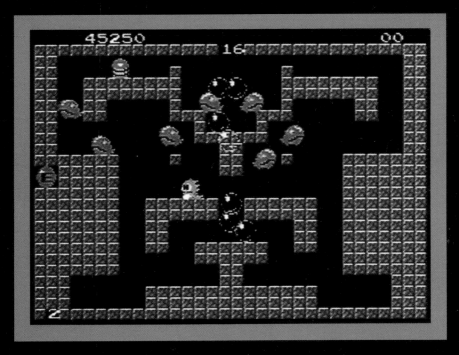

Manufactured by Taito Software, Inc. Bub and Bob, bubble-blowing Brontosauruses, explore a series of mazes to find their two friends who were kidnapped by Baron von Blubba.

Arcade-style action game with clever monsters and lots of bubble-popping fun.

With the possible exceptions of Lolo and Lala in the *Adventures of Lolo 1 and 2,* video game heroes don't come any cuter than Bub, the bubble-blow-ing Brontosaurus in *Bubble Bobble.* Yes, that green thing with the bewildered look on its face is supposed to be a Brontosaurus. Never mind that it looks more like a cross between a Tyrannosaurus, a Stegosaurus, and a muppet.

Bub (and his friend Bob, if you have a second controller and a second player) is looking for his kidnapped friends. To find them, he has to wander through two worlds made up of 113 mazes apiece. This is a big game and a tough one!

Move Bub around the mazes with the arrow buttons. To blow a bubble, press the B button. To jump, press A. Blowing bubbles is the only way to catch the monsters. Once a monster is surrounded by a bubble, you can jump on top of it and convert it into a bonus item, such as a piece of fruit. Different bonus items have different point values. Some, such as candy, will even give Bub special powers. The candy gives him the ability to blow more bubbles, and over longer distances.

TIPS & TRICKS

- In most mazes, you don't have to seek out the monsters. They'll be happy to come to you. Just lie in wait and blow bubbles at them as soon as they come in range.
- You can finish the game with only one player, but you'll need two to have a happy ending—honest.

- Jump on top of the blue bubbles and you'll get a fast ride through the maze. This is a good way to get a lot of bonus items in a hurry, but look out for monsters!
- Some bubbles have letters of the alphabet in them. If you can pop the bubbles that spell the word EX-TEND, you can jump ahead as much as five levels.

BACKDOORS & PASSWORDS

We're not suggesting you cheat or anything, but here's the password that will take you to the last screen of the first world: EECJJ. And if that's not enough for you, this one will get you to the end of the game: EECFG.

CONTRA

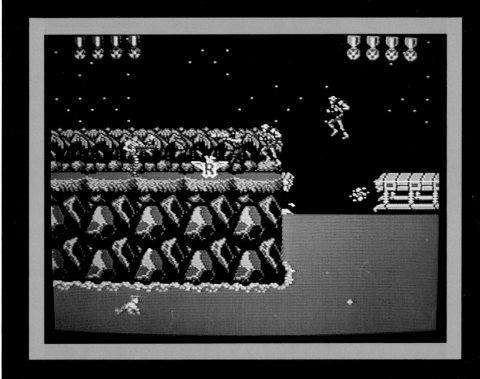

Manufactured by Konami Inc. A Rambo-like American mercenary repels an alien invasion deep in the South American jungles, fighting soldiers, flying saucers—and monsters!

QUICK REVIEW

Ultrafast game for players who like action, action, and—for a little variety—more action.

HOW IT WORKS

If you read the newspapers, you might expect a game called *Contra* to be about guerrilla fighting in South America. In fact, this game looks a lot more like the Arnold Schwarzenegger movie *Predator,* where mercenary soldiers battle creatures from another planet.

Move your soldier with the left and right arrow buttons. Aim your weapon at the sky with the up arrow and drop to the ground with the down arrow. The B button fires your weapon and the A button sends you leaping into the air.

On the first level, you run horizontally along the ground, past jungles and ocean, shooting at the hordes of soldiers who come running at you and the flying saucers that occasionally swoop down out of the sky. On the second level, you'll run down long corridors, shooting your way through strange barricades. Then you'll climb a series of cliffs alongside a waterfall, dodging bullets every step of the way. Finally, you'll fight giant tanks in an endless arctic snowfield.

At the end of every level, a boss machine or monster will attempt to demolish you with bullets and energy weapons. Keep shooting at this character until it explodes.

TIPS & TRICKS

- Bridges have a tendency to blow up when you try to cross them. Just before you reach the bridge, do a forward flip by hitting the A button while holding down the right arrow. Then keep flipping across the bridge just ahead of the explosions.
- If you see a crowd of enemy soldiers heading toward you, drop to the ground and shoot from a prone position. As long as the enemy is on the same level you are, their bullets can't hit you. But watch out for soldiers above and below you!
- When you shoot a flying saucer, an eagle insignia will appear. Pick it up, and you'll have a powerful alien weapon to use against the enemy!
- At the end of the first level, you'll come up against a high wall full of deadly weapons. There are four things you can shoot at here: the soldier at the top, the two cannon in the middle, and the glowing disc at the bottom. But you can get through the wall just by shooting at the glowing disc until it explodes.

- While running down the underground corridors, always shoot at the glowing red discs first. Lots of barricades will self-destruct as soon as you get rid of the glowing disc, no matter what other targets may be in the way.
- When you come face to face with the boss alien at the top of the waterfall, shoot at its arms first. Then aim for the head.
- The boss monster with the four constantly shifting heads can only be destroyed if you shoot at the points where its heads come together. It doesn't take many shots, but be careful to dodge all the flying weapons while you're shooting!
- The giant tanks in the snowfield look indestructible. But if you lie flat on the ground and keep shooting at them, you'll eventually finish them off.

BACKDOORS & PASSWORDS

If *Contra* is too tough for you, try this trick to get some extra lives: When you see the Player Select screen, rapidly press up, up, down, down, left, right, left, right, A, B, and START. When the game starts, you'll have thirty men! And you'll get thirty more men for each of your two continues, for a total of ninety men. That should keep you playing for a while!

DOUBLE DRAGON II: THE REVENGE

Manufactured by Tradewest Inc. Martial arts masters Billy and Jimmy Lee are the last good guys left in New York after nuclear war has reduced the world to rubble. Now they're out to stop the advance of the vicious Black Shadow Warriors.

QUICK REVIEW

Challenging enough for experts, but with a practice mode to get beginners into the action, this is an excellent Kung-fu chop'em'up!

HOW IT WORKS

Double Dragon II is divided into eight missions, each one tougher than the one before. You play Billy Lee, the martial arts master from the original *Double Dragon.* If you have a second game controller, a friend can play Billy Lee's brother Jimmy.

The evil Black Shadow Warriors have killed your girlfriend Marian, and you're out for revenge. *Double Dragon II* takes you from the mean streets of post-nuclear New York up to the top of several buildings and on a helicopter ride to a mysterious island. There, you'll work your way through the Undersea Base, the Mansion of Terror, and the Trap Room. Finally, you'll have to beat the Double Illusion, two martial arts masters who look just like Jimmy and Billy Lee!

There are three different levels of play in *Double Dragon II:* Practice, Warrior, and Supreme Master. If you play at the Practice level, you'll only be allowed to finish the first three missions. At the Supreme Master level, though, you'll get a special ninth mission: the Final Confrontation, where you'll meet the mastermind of the Shadow Warriors. There's also a special mode where Billy and Jimmy Lee can fight one another as well as the villains!

TIPS & TRICKS

- The villains in this game like to gang up on you in pairs. Knock one out fast, then punch the other one before the first one can regain consciousness.
- The mini-boss in the metal mask at the end of Mission One is a tough customer—if you let him get close enough to grab you. Keep him at arm's length with a rapid volley of punches.
- When fighting in high places (something you'll spend a lot of time doing in this game), stay away from ledges. An otherwise harmless punch that knocks you off a ledge can sub-

tract one life from your character's inventory. On the other hand, knocking the villains off ledges is a good way to win a fight in a hurry.
- As soon as you get to the top of the building at the beginning of Mission Two, a helicopter filled with bad guys will come swooping and disgorge its contents onto the roof. If you're standing on the roof when it arrives, the chopper will blow you away with gunfire. Unfortunately, the chopper won't show up until you reach the roof, so climb the ladder, take a quick peek at the roof, and get back down as soon as you hear the sound of gunfire.
- Inside the helicopter in Mission Three, there is a powerful wind current that pulls you toward the exit door every time it opens up. You'll have to fight against this while keeping the villains at bay. Try to stay on the left side of your foes so that they'll get pulled out the door before you do!
- Make things easier for yourself by getting a friend to play along as Jimmy Lee. You can win with only one player, but it won't be easy.

DUCK TALES

AT A GLANCE

Manufactured by Capcom USA Inc. Scrooge McDuck, the world's richest duck, is out to make himself even richer by traveling around the world (and to the Moon!) to find hidden treasure. The game is based on the *Duck Tales* TV show.

QUICK REVIEW

Clever graphics and a solid plot make this a pleasing action-filled game with a touch of adventure.

HOW IT WORKS

When the game begins, you'll see Scrooge McDuck's computerized Control Panel, which gives you a choice of five places that you can visit. Use the up and down arrows to choose between the Amazon, Transylvania, the African Mines, the Himalayas, and the Moon. Push the A button to enter your choice.

Once you arrive at your destination, you can move back and forth with the left and right arrows, jump with the A button, and swing your cane with the B button. Pushing the down arrow button causes Scrooge to—you should excuse the expression—duck.

The real secret to traveling through these exotic lands, however, is the pogo jump. This is a tricky maneuver to pull off and requires a lot of practice, but once you get the hang of it, you'll use it through most of the game.

To do the pogo jump, press the A button for a normal jump, then quickly press the down arrow and the B button. Scrooge will start pogoing and will keep on pogoing for as long as you keep pressing the B button. To pogo left and right as well as up and down, use the left and right arrows.

At the top of the screen, you'll see Scrooge's score (which tells you how much money he's made on his travels), the number of hit points (HP) that Scrooge has left (when the hit points run out, Scrooge loses a life), the number of lives he has left (you'll start with three), and the number of seconds left to explore.

There is a special treasure hidden in each of these distant lands. Along the way to the treasure, you'll find diamonds, food, and magic coins. The diamonds increase Scrooge's money. The food increases his hit points. (Ice cream cones give him one point and cake heals him completely.) Magic coins, which look like circles with an M in the middle, make him invulnerable for a few seconds. There are other surprise goodies, too, including miniature Uncle Scrooge dolls that will give you extra lives!

Somewhere in each land you'll run into Scrooge's faithful pilot, Launchpad McQuack, who'll offer to take you back to Duckburg where you can put your new-found riches in the bank. After you've located all the treasures, prepare for a battle with a tough boss monster.

TIPS & TRICKS

- Learn to do the pogo jump as soon as you can; you won't get far without it. There are places Scrooge can't go and things he can't do if he can't pogo.
- When you find a chest or other object that you can't open, pogo on top of it. It'll pop open and its contents will come out. Pogoing is also a good way to smash rocks, which sometimes have jewels and other goodies hidden inside.
- Use the pogo jump to get Scrooge across pointy objects that would injure him if he crossed them on foot.
- The best, and safest, way to get rid of your enemies is to pogo on top of them. But be sure not to miss, because they'll take a whack out of you if you do!
- If you find an object wedged in a tight place and you want to examine it, hit it with your cane. Sometimes this will knock the object down where you can get at it. But it doesn't always work.

- When the roof is too low for you to pogo on top of one of the bad guys, look for an object lying on the floor and hit it with your cane. If you aim correctly at the face, you'll send him flying!
- In Transylvania, Huey will tell you there's an "illusion wall" somewhere in the castle. Actually, there are *two* illusion walls. Walk up to these walls and you'll go right through them! Unfortunately, there's no way to tell an illusion wall from a normal wall just by looking at it (which is probably why they call it an illusion wall).
- You can't pogo on top of a ghost. Just use the down arrow button to crouch where the ghost can't touch you, and it'll pass you by.
- After Scrooge loses a life, his image on the screen will seem to flicker for a few seconds. While he's flickering, he can't be hurt, so take advantage of the situation and slip past particularly nasty enemies while Scrooge is flashing on and off!

BACKDOORS & PASSWORDS

If you ask Launchpad to take you back to Duckburg when you have a score of between 70,000 and 79,999, you'll enter a special bonus round, where you can jump through the clouds and gather all the diamonds you can pick up.

FASCINATING FACTOIDS

The *Duck Tales* cartoon show is based on a series of comic books written and drawn between 1943 and 1966 by a former Disney animator named Carl Barks. Many of the original comic books are now rare—and expensive—collectors' items.

AT A GLANCE

Manufactured by Techmo Inc. A Ninja warrior named Ryu comes to America to avenge the death of his father. A sideways-scrolling martial arts game.

QUICK REVIEW

Enough action to put blisters on your playing fingers. The graphics are just okay, but the jumping and sword-fighting are top-notch.

HOW IT WORKS

Press the A button to make your Ninja jump, the B button to make him fight. When you leap at a wall, you'll cling to it, like Spiderman. When there are two walls across from each other, you can climb them by leaping back and forth between them.

The game is divided into six stages, or "acts," separated by animation sequences that gradually reveal the story behind the game. In the beginning, if you pause for a moment before pushing the START button, you'll see Ryu's father murdered by a mysterious Ninja warrior. Ryu then receives a posthumous message from his dad telling him to go to America and seek out an Indiana Jones–like archaeologist named Walter Smith.

The action begins in the fictional American city of Galesburg, with Ryu-jumping and slicing his way through hordes of criminals, bullies, guard dogs, and (of course) Ninja warriors. (The streets that Ryu fights his way down don't resemble any neighborhoods the author of this book has ever seen outside of B-rated kung-fu movies, but maybe this is what Japanese programmers think American cities look like.) At the end of this first act you enter Jay's bar, where you meet the mysterious Irene Lew. Irene leads you into Act Two, where you fight still more Ninja warriors as you make your way across Death Valley.

In Act Three you meet Walter Smith and battle your way across a desert lake, through mountains, and deep into a cavern. Then, in Act Four, Walter Smith is murdered, and the CIA joins in the chase; you find yourself in the Amazon jungle and in a temple battling demons. In Act Five you climb a pyramid, and in Act Six you go one on one against the unbeatable (?) warrior Jaquio, who murdered your father.

TIPS & TRICKS

- The Barbarian boss at the end of the first level looks tough, but he really isn't. Push the controller down and go into a crouch, where he can't hit you. Then chop at him until he explodes in a burst of flame!
- There are lamps on the wall in some screens. Chop at them with

your weapon, and you'll find that they contain special bonus items, some of which give your warriors extra powers.

- To use an extra power, press the B button and the up arrow at the same time.
- The Firewheel item gives Ryu Firewheel power, with three balls of fire twirling around his head, zapping everybody he comes close to. It only lasts for about ten seconds, so move fast when the fireballs start to whirl!
- Wall jumping is the only way to get Ryu through most of the screens in this game. It's easy to do. Jump against a wall, and Ryu will stick to it like a fly on flypaper. Then jump again, and he'll cling to any other walls he hits. Many bonus items are located so high above the ground that this may be the only way that you can reach them. It's also the only way to climb many of the vertical passageways in the game.
- One of the special bonus items gives Ryu the "jump and slash technique." Use it by jumping into the air and pressing the B button. You'll need it to win some of the big battles in the game.
- Basaquer, the boss at the end of Act Three, will fire bullets at you. Knock them aside with your sword,

then go for him when he lands on the ground to your left.

BACKDOORS & PASSWORDS

When the title screen comes on, press A, B, and SELECT all at the same time, then press START. You'll enter a special sound test mode.

FASCINATING FACTOIDS

The Japanese word *gaiden* means "telegram" or "message." At the beginning of the game, the Ninja Ryu receives a message from his late father telling him to go to America. Hence, the title means, roughly, "Ninja message."

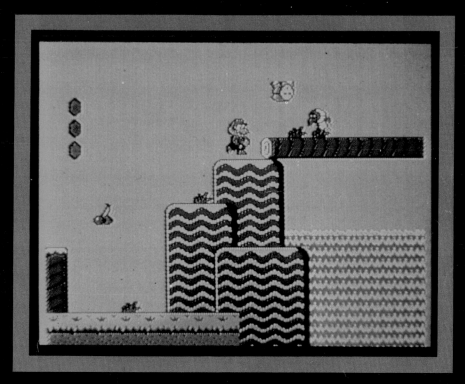

AT A GLANCE

Manufactured by Nintendo of America Inc. Mario the carpenter runs and jumps to save the dream world of Subcon from the evil Wart.

QUICK REVIEW

One of the very best games in the all-time greatest series of running-and-jumping style video games. Loads of fun!

HOW IT WORKS

Mario the carpenter, formerly of *Super Mario Brothers* and *Donkey Kong,* has a dream about a strange land called Subcon and then finds himself in Sub-con for real. Mario must fight his way past armies of bizarre and sometimes ridiculous enemies to defeat the evil Wart.

You move Mario (or his friends Luigi, Princess Toadstool, and Toad) with the directional controller. Press the B button to make him pick things up and the A button to jump.

TIPS & TRICKS

- Pick up every little tuft of grass that you can. Some will turn out to be vegetables, which you can throw at your enemies to knock them off the screen. Others may be potions, which will open the door to the subworld, which usually contains mushrooms that will give you extra lives. Still others will turn out to be clocks, which will stop time while you dance on your enemies!

■ How do you get past the dinosaur-like bird who spits eggs at you at the end of several worlds? When he spits an egg at you, jump on top of the egg, grab it with the B button, and throw it right back at him. Do this three times and the bird will vanish, leaving behind the football-like object that he was holding. Jump on it and pick it up, and you'll get a pleasant surprise (along with a nifty bit of animation).

■ If you've picked up some coins in a world, you'll get a chance to play a slot machine at the end of that world. Slot combinations that begin with one or more cherries and any three-in-a-row combination will win you extra lives. Here's a trick that may help you get ahead: the second symbol to come up in the first window after the slots start spinning is always a cherry. Hit the A button quickly enough and you can dependably win at least one extra life on every spin.

■ Pidgit, the bird on a flying carpet, will greet you at the beginning of World 1-2. Jump up just as he swoops down at you and land on his head. Use the B button to pick Pidgit up off the carpet. Then use the directional controller to fly on your way. Be careful, though, that you don't jump on the carpet while it's slightly below ground level; you won't be able to fly it. You'll have to jump back to the previous hill so that Pidgit will come back and give you another chance.

■ Once you're done with Pidgit, grab the first tuft of grass that you see. It's a potion. Enter the subworld, then come back out and enter the first vase on your right. There's a one-up (which will give you extra strength) at the bottom of it. Exit this vase and enter another vase. You'll find a key at the bottom. Grab the key and get out as fast as you can. Phanto will be on your trail until you make it through the next door. If Phanto gets too close, simply drop the key. He'll vanish, and he won't come back until you pick it up again.

■ Halfway through World 1-3 you'll come to a tall shaft lined with green girders and green bricks. Go all the way to the top of the shaft and enter the door you find there. Take the key from the room behind the door. Once again, Phanto will begin chasing you. Go back down the shaft, dropping the key whenever you need to get Phanto off your tail. (Be sure to drop it *only* when there's something underneath it to catch it!) Stay toward the right side of the shaft and at the bottom you'll find a door.

■ At the end of World 1–3, you'll meet Mouser, a bomb-throwing mouse. Give him a taste of his own medicine. You'll need three bombs to get Mouser out of the way, but don't blow yourself up in the process!

SUPER MARIO BROTHERS 3

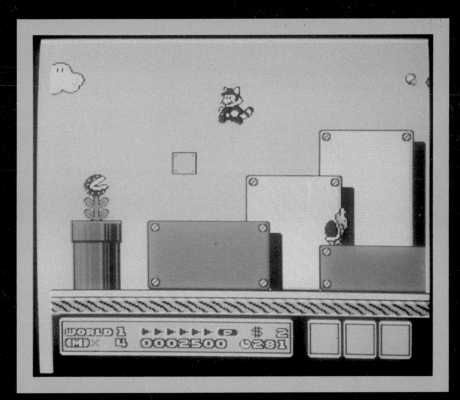

AT A GLANCE

Manufactured by Nintendo of America Inc. Mario and friend fight to rescue the Mushroom Kingdom from the evil Bowser and his seven children.

QUICK REVIEW

The best (and most popular) running-and-jumping game around!

HOW IT WORKS

Mario (along with his brother Luigi, if you've got a second player) is sent by Princess Toadstool to rescue the once-peaceful Mushroom Kingdom from Bowser, the evil king of the Koopas.

Mario is more "super" than ever this time out. Now he can fly when he runs fast enough and don various animal suits to gain special powers. This is the most complex and fascinating *Mario* game yet!

TIPS & TRICKS

▪ Be sure to read the manual extra carefully. There are lots of stunts that Mario can pull in this game, many of which he wasn't capable of in earlier games. Flying is a particularly valuable trick and can be used to gather all sorts of extra treasures and power-ups.

▪ Not all of the action in *Super Mario 3* is on the ground. Much of it is up in the sky, where you can't see it until you get Mario off the ground. Make a habit of flying around wherever there's enough running space for Mario to manage a take-off and checking for surprises that can't normally be seen.

■ Turtles are valuable objects. They can be used to break open objects that Mario can't break open himself. When you see a turtle, look around to see if there isn't something you can break open by jumping on the turtle, grabbing it, and letting it go.

■ The first action scene in World One is chockful of surprises and goodies. It's a good place to get acquainted with the game and learn what you can expect in later worlds. Here are some things you should try in this scene:

□ The fourth question block from the entrance contains a power-up mushroom. Hit it from underneath, grab the mushroom, and turn little Mario into Super Mario.

□ Jump on the first turtle, grab it, and hurl it toward the next question block on the right. A power-up feather or mushroom will pop out. If Mario is already Super Mario, the feather will turn him into Raccoon Mario.

□ Now that Mario is Raccoon Mario, he can fly! Jump on the three approaching monsters to clear the path, move Mario as far to the left as he can go without crossing a question block, run rapidly to the right with the B button pressed down, and start flapping his arms with the A button as soon as the P symbol at the bottom of the screen lights up. Mario will soar into the sky, where you'll find coins galore, several floating platforms, and a brick containing a one-up mushroom (which will give Mario an additional life).

□ When Mario gets back to earth, he'll see two piles of bricks, one large and one small, with a turtle walking back and forth on top of the second block. If Mario still has his raccoon tail, use it to knock off the three blocks on the right side of the first pile. (Otherwise, toss the turtle to the left, and he'll shatter the appropriate bricks; in fact, you might want to do this the first time to learn which bricks to break.) There will be an overhanging brick left over. Hit it from underneath and a switch block will appear on top of it. Jump on the switch block and all the bricks will turn to coins.

□ At the end of the level, don't grab the card symbol right away. Instead, go to the far right, then start running to the left until Mario flies. (He'll need his raccoon suit for this.) Fly up the long pipe and enter it from the top. You'll find a bonanza of coins inside.

▫ Remember what you did in this first action scene, because a lot of the later scenes allow you to try similar stunts—and a few that are even wilder!

■ There's a shortcut that will get you to the end of the third action scene in World One. Just after you enter the scene, you'll see a large structure made of bricks with a turtle on top. Jump on the turtle and toss him to the left. He'll break some of the bricks and slide away. Stand beside the question block on the left end of the structure and jump into the air. A jump block will appear. Leap on it and press the A button. You'll soar high into the air and land on a cloud. Gather the pennies you find on the cloud, slide down the pipe at the end of the cloud, and you'll be at the end of Scene Three.

■ Yes, Virginia, there is a warp whistle, just like it says in the manual. It's in Scene Three of World One. Near the end of the scene, you'll find seven floating platforms in a row. (If you've taken the shortcut, you'll have to double back to find them.) Jump on top of the third platform from the left.

It should be white in color. Have Mario crouch down for about ten seconds. (He'll need to be at least Super Mario in order to crouch.) He'll fall through the cloud and will now be able to walk BEHIND the scenery! Move quickly to the end of the level, where Mario will go behind the black goal screen. He'll find himself in a room of Toad's house, with one chest in the middle. Open the chest and get the warp whistle. You can use the warp whistle from the map screen. It will take Mario to the Warp Zone, where he can choose to go to the Second, Third, or Fourth Worlds!

■ Here's one of the strangest things we've found in this or any other Nintendo game: If you complete certain action scenes, including Scene One of World One, while the number of coins that you are carrying is evenly divisible by 11 *and* the second digit from the right in the number of coins is the same as the second digit from the right in your score *and* you grab a card while the time clock is on an even number, the Hammer Brother on the current map will turn into a ship! (For example, if you have 99 coins, your score is 6190, and the timer reads 162 when you grab a card, then you've nailed it!) When you board the ship, you'll get a bonus round, where you can grab as many coins as you can carry. But you'll still have to fight the Hammer Brothers when you're done!

■ When the ceiling in the mini-castle of World One starts descending on you, don't panic. Just look for a spot where there's a notch in the ceiling and stand there until it goes back up again.

FASCINATING FACTOIDS

The *Super Mario* games are the creation of Shigeru Miyamoto, the same game designer who created the *Zelda* adventures for Nintendo.

TEENAGE
MUTANT NINJA
TURTLES

AT A GLANCE

Manufactured by Ultra Software Corp. Four hard-shelled martial artists go head to head with the vicious Shredder and his dreaded Toe Clan. Chop and sock your way through dozens of horizontally scrolling screens of action.

QUICK REVIEW

Classy martial arts game with great graphics, fast action, and a musical score that will have you dancing while you play.

HOW IT WORKS

Use the directional controller to guide the turtles, one at a time, along the platforms and ladders. Pressing the START button during the action lets you switch turtles, read a playing hint, look at a map of the city, or just catch your breath. To make the current turtle use his weapon, press B; to jump, press A. There are pizzas and extra weapons scattered all over the place. Grabbing a pizza restores your energy.

The game is divided into three levels. You'll explore buildings and sewers. You'll even swim through a lake to stop Shredder from blowing up a dam!

TIPS & TRICKS

- Get to know your turtles! Each has a different weapon and different strengths:

Michelangelo (Mike) is weak, but he can take out a lot of small attackers with one swing of his blade.

Donatello (Don) is slow but strong, and his weapon reaches the farthest distance of all.

Leonardo (Leo) is weak, but he can reach almost as far as Donatello.

Raphael (Raph) is the fastest and jumps the highest.

■ Don't be afraid to switch turtles when you need to. For instance, let Donatello fight the pig-faced mini-boss at the end of the second sewer. But don't let the boss get too close to him, or Don will get his shell squashed!

■ There are cars and other vehicles on the surface that will run you over if you wander too far from the sewers and buildings that you're supposed to be checking out. Just stay out of their way. They're more of an annoyance than a real threat. Probably, the programmers just wanted to make sure you spend most of your time underground or in the buildings, where the action is.

■ When you see a pizza, hit the START button and check to see which of your turtles is weakest. Don't waste all those extra energy points on a turtle who is already at full strength!

■ Some sewers have pizzas near the beginning or end. If you eat the pizzas, leave the sewer, and then re-enter it, the pizzas will magically reappear. This is a good way to heal your worn-out turtles. Just keep going back to the sewer and eating pizzas until everyone is in tiptop shape.

■ Learn to leap and fight at the same time; it's the best way to defeat enemies who come flying at you from above.

■ Can't find all of the bombs when swimming behind the dam? You'll have to swim through a wall of deadly weeds to get the last three. Don't worry, though. There's a narrow path through the weeds. But you might lose a few points along the way, so don't send a weak turtle to do the job.

■ Don't let the current turtle run out of points while swimming, or you'll have to start again from the point where you jumped off the dam! This can be a major problem, especially if you've already gotten past the seaweed. Switch turtles fast when the current one gets weak.

■ Learn to keep your swimming turtles from sinking to the bottom. This isn't all that important most of the time, but if there's seaweed on the bottom your turtle may conk out before you can get him back in the swim.

The pizza-munching turtles originally appeared in a black and white comic book that debuted in 1985. They were so popular that they immediately spawned imitators with colorful names such as *Armor-Plated Adolescent Aardvarks!*

The first names of the turtles—Michelangelo, Raphael, Leonardo, and Donatello—are the names of Italian Renaissance artists who lived between 1386 and 1564. The movie based on the turtles is the most popular film of all time despite the fact that it wasn't released either in summer or at Christmas.

TETRIS

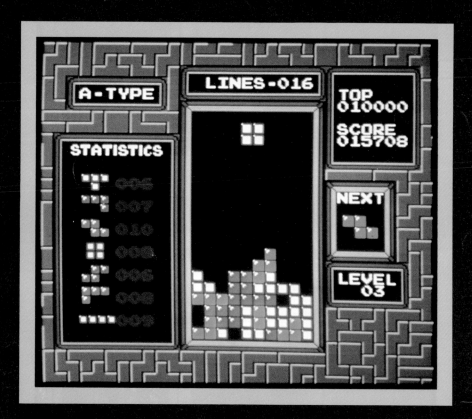

AT A GLANCE

Manufactured by Nintendo of America Inc. The sky is falling! Put the pieces together to form solid lines of blocks and win points!

QUICK REVIEW

One of the simplest and most fascinating strategy games ever invented! Just as it's impossible to eat only one peanut, nobody can play just one game of *Tetris!*

HOW IT WORKS

A variety of geometric shapes are falling out of the sky, and it's your job to guide them into neat rows on the ground. When you complete a solid row of shapes, it will be removed from the screen, and your score will increase.

The left and right buttons guide the shapes back and forth. When you're ready to move the shape down to the ground, push the down arrow—or just wait for the shape to get there by itself. Push the A button to rotate the shape in a clockwise direction and the B to rotate it counterclockwise.

Removing more than one row at a time will gain you bonus points. Removing four rows at once nets you a Tetris, the maximum point grabber!

The Nintendo version of *Tetris* features two different types of games. Type A is the normal *Tetris* game. Type B is a special tournament where you have to stack the shapes sixteen rows high without having the completed rows removed from the stack!

this as a guide for positioning the current shape. Don't block gaps that the next shape might fit inside!

TIPS & TRICKS

- The rows that you fill in don't have to be at the bottom of the screen. They can be anywhere in the pile. If there are holes you can't reach because of the pieces on top of them, see if you can't remove the rows that are in your way.
- The long, straight shape is the most useful one in *Tetris,* because it can be used to fill the long gaps that no other shape will fit. And, it's the only shape that will get you a Tetris! Unfortunately, it's also the rarest shape, so don't depend on one showing up when you need it. Learn to fit the more awkward shapes into awkwardly shaped holes.
- Try not to leave gaps along the side of the pile. These are the hardest to fill in. Build your pile from the outside in, leaving small gaps in the middle.
- A tiny window on the right side of the screen shows you the next shape, the one that hasn't appeared yet. Use

FASCINATING FACTOIDS

Tetris was invented by Russian programmer Alexey Pajitnov. It's the first computer game from the Soviet Union to become a best seller in the United States.

Tetris offers you a choice of four different musical scores to accompany the game. The first, and most beautiful, of the scores is from the classical ballet *The Nutcracker,* written by nineteenth-century Russian composer Peter Ilich Tchaikovsky.

Originally, there were two versions of the *Tetris* video game available for play on the Nintendo Entertainment System, one from Nintendo, the other from Tengen. But Nintendo, claiming to have exclusive American rights to the game, took Tengen to court and won, so the Tengen version is no longer available for sale (though you might find it for rent). Some game experts believe that the Tengen version is even better than the Nintendo!

Manufactured by Capcom USA Inc. Pilot a P-38 fighter plane through wave after wave of attacking enemy planes and ships to win the World War II Battle of Midway.

QUICK REVIEW

A solid old-fashioned shoot'em'up game, but probably the weirdest version of a World War II battle you'll ever see!

HOW IT WORKS

Grab your controller (or, better still, a joystick) and guide your P-38 over a constantly scrolling ocean. The screen moves forward only, but you can use the directional controller to move your airplane a tiny ways backward, forward, left, or right. Push the B button to fire your current weapon and the A button to zap all of the enemies on the screen at once with a giant lightning bolt.

Your P-38 has a limited amount of energy. You'll see it tick away while you fly and vanish even faster when enemy gunfire hits you or you collide with an enemy plane. But special POW symbols will appear on the screen every now and then that can be used to POWer-up your airplane. When the POW symbols appear, shoot at them. They'll change into other symbols.

Some of these symbols will give you extra power; others will give you special weapons. Learn to recognize which symbols are which, so you can get what you need.

At the end of each wave, you'll face off against a giant airplane or ship and get a bonus if you can polish it off. When this boss machine is destroyed, special bonus figures such as cows, cats, or astronauts will appear. Cows and astronauts in a game about the Battle of Midway? We told you this game was weird!

TIPS & TRICKS

- A flight of pink airplanes will appear every now and then from one of the sides of the screen. If you shoot *every* plane in the flight, a POW symbol will appear. In the later stages of the game, you'll need to get every one of these symbols in order to keep flying.
- Shoot at clouds. Sometimes they have bonus symbols hidden inside them!
- Try to keep your P-38 about two-thirds of the way down from the top of the screen. That'll give you time to maneuver when a squadron of enemy planes appears at the top of the screen but will keep you from getting caught by surprise when planes fly out from behind you.
- When an airplane or a ship near your P-38 starts to blow up, get away from it fast! The explosion will do damage to your own plane and lower your energy points.
- Sometimes you'll notice a slight twinkling in the sky in front of your plane. Start shooting at it and keep on shooting. It's an invisible plane, and you can get bonus points for blowing it up.

BACKDOORS & PASSWORDS

Does your P-38 keep getting shot out of the sky? Here's the password for Wave 23, the last one in the game: TY19U.

FASCINATING FACTOIDS

The real Battle of Midway was fought in June of 1942, yet the name of this game is *1943*. Could the programmers be writing about a war that took place in a parallel universe where cows and astronauts inhabit ships in the Pacific Ocean—and the Battle of Midway took place a year later than it actually did?

The Battle of Midway was a cataclysmic defeat for the Japanese armed forces, who were fighting the Americans in World War II. Yet this game was published by Capcom, a Japanese gamemaker. It's nice to know that they have no hard feelings half a century later.

Notice, however, that the game never either names the country you're fighting for or the country you're fighting against!

RECOMMENDED READING

Want to learn more about Nintendo? Here's a list of books and magazines full of hints, tips, and game descriptions similar to the ones in this book:

Robbins, Judd, and Joshua Robbins. *Mastering Nintendo Video Games: Tips, Tricks, Strategies.* Hayden Books. Indianapolis, 1989.

Rovin, Jeff. *How to Win at Nintendo Games, Vols. 1, 2 and 3.* St. Martin's Paperbacks. New York, 1988, 1989, 1990.

Sandler, Corey, and Tom Badgett. *Ultimate Unauthorized Nintendo Game Strategies, Vols. 1 and 2.* Bantam. New York, 1989, 1990.

Schwarz, Steven. *Compute's Guide to Nintendo Games.* Compute! Books. Radnor, Pennsylvania, 1989.

Electronic Gaming Monthly. Sendai Publications Inc. Lombard, Illinois. $3.95 a copy. U.S. subscriptions $19.95 per year.

Game Player's. Signal Research, Inc. Greensboro, North Carolina. $2.95 a copy. U.S. subscriptions $17.95 per year.

GamePro. IDG Communications/Peterborough, Inc. Peterborough, New Hampshire. $3.95 a copy. U.S. subscriptions $24.95 per year.

Nintendo Power, Nintendo of America, Inc. Redmond, Washington. $3.50 a copy. U.S. subscriptions $21 per year.

Video Games & Computer Entertainment. L.F.P., Inc. Beverly Hills, California. $2.95 a copy. U.S. subscriptions $19.95 per year.

INDEX